# Ballet

CONTENTS


The Magic of Ballet ....................2
In a Class of Your Own ..............4
Dressed for Dance .....................6
Ready to Dance ..........................8
At the Barre .............................10
In the Centre ...........................12
Jumps .......................................14
Sur les Pointes .........................16
Ballet History ...........................18
Great Teachers .........................20
Famous Dancers ......................22
Old Favourites .........................24
Creating New Ballet .................26
Style on Stage ..........................28
It's Showtime ...........................30


CollinsChildren'sBooks

# The Magic of Ballet

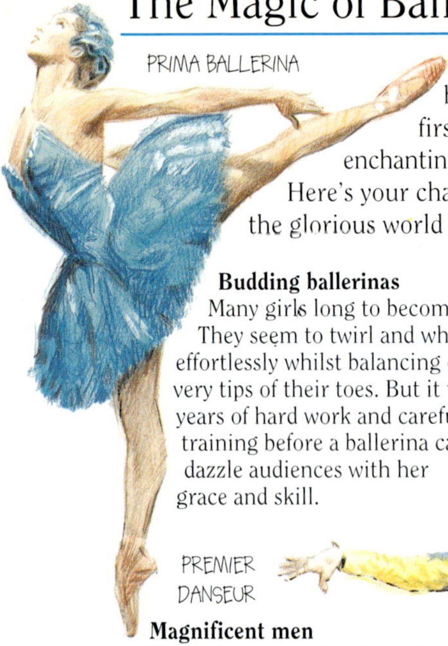

PRIMA BALLERINA

Watching ballet for the first time is an enchanting experience. Here's your chance to enter the glorious world of ballet.

**Budding ballerinas**

Many girls long to become ballerinas. They seem to twirl and whirl so effortlessly whilst balancing on the very tips of their toes. But it takes years of hard work and careful training before a ballerina can dazzle audiences with her grace and skill.

PREMIER DANSEUR

**Magnificent men**

Young boys envy the strength and energy of any premier danseur (male principal). He can hold a ballerina in the air with one hand and jump so high, that he seems to be almost flying!

## THE CORPS DE BALLET

The dancers in the corps de ballet (which means the body of ballet) must all be the same height. They learn to dance together, with perfect timing. The effect of members of the corps de ballet moving as one person can be quite magical.

## WHAT A PERFORMANCE!

- In 1988 the British dancer Wayne Sleep completed 158 jumps (grands jetés) in just two minutes!
- Dame Margot Fonteyn and Rudolph Nureyev received a staggering 89 curtain calls in Austria in 1964 after a triumphant performance of *Swan Lake*.
- The largest-ever cast of 2,000 ballet dancers went on stage at the Royal Albert Hall in London in 1962.
- Principal dancers get through about twelve pairs of ballet shoes every month.

# In a Class of Your Own

'Class' is probably the most widely-used word in a ballet dancer's vocabulary! No dancer, however famous, can survive without a daily class.

*A class in progress at the Paris Opéra. This school was founded back in 1713.*

***Where?***
If you need help tracking down a good class near where you live, get yourself a copy of a specialist dance magazine. Or you could contact the Council for Dance Education and Training (UK), Riverside Studios, Crisp Road, London W6.

***... and when?***
It's fun to start dancing at a very early age, when your body is flexible enough to adapt to the demands of ballet. But wait until you are eight or nine for more serious training. There's an exception to every rule! Rudolph Nureyev didn't start serious ballet training until he was 16 and went on to become the most famous male dancer in the world!

**A size guide**
Ballet dancers have to be the right height: not too tall and not too short! Girls should be 1.57–1.63m and boys 1.63–1.88m. Male dancers should always be taller than their partners!

## KNOW YOUR FRENCH!

In every country where ballet is taught, the steps are known by their French names. Here are just a few:

| | |
|---|---|
| Plier | to bend |
| Tendu | stretched |
| Sauter | to spring |
| Ports de bras | arm exercise |
| Jeter | to throw |
| Poser | to step |
| Relever | to rise |
| A terre | on the ground |

*Many ballet classes are held in school or church halls, rather than purpose-built studios.*

**Floor facts**

The dance floor must be smooth, clean and not slippery. Lightly sprinkling the floor with water and rubbing shoes into a sticky powder called rosin helps prevent slipping.

**Exams**

Exams give you a goal to work towards and help mark your progress. Different teaching societies devise their own set of exams. Exams may be nail-biting but it is a wonderful feeling to receive your first ballet certificate!

**Your teacher**

Some dancers decide early in their career to concentrate on teaching. They take a special training course. But many teachers have been dancers themselves (sometimes very famous ones). They have turned to teaching when their performing career is over. Ballet teachers, male or female, can be any age – and any size!

# Dressed for Dance

You need to look the part for your ballet class. Dance clothes are designed to give great freedom of movement and also to allow the teacher to see pupils' bodies clearly in order to correct their positions.

**His 'n' hers**

Girls wear leotards, with tights or socks. They may have a little skirt to hold. Small boys start ballet wearing trunks and a T-shirt and socks. Later they wear tights too.

## SHOES

Ballet shoes must fit 'like a glove'. (Never leave room to grow!) 'Soft' or 'flat' shoes are worn by everyone at first. Later on girls wear 'pointe' shoes. Shoes are made from leather, canvas or satin and come in lots of different colours.

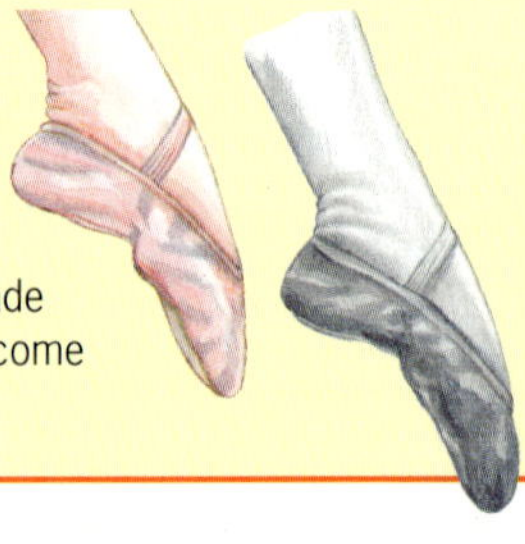

## HAIR

2

Every bit of a dancer must be tidy in class, especially the hair. If hair is not long enough, or time is short, it may be hard to make a proper 'chignon'. The important thing is to keep your hair off the face and neck, so a pony tail or bunches would do the trick. Boys' hair must be kept short.

1

3

**Old timers**

In days gone by, girls wore tunics for class. Wouldn't these pupils from the 1950s be amazed to see the ballet clothes worn today?

**Keeping warm**

Dancers, like athletes, must keep their bodies warm to avoid injuring muscles. At the start of class, especially on a cold day, dancers do not look very elegant in leg warmers, cardigans, extra socks and sometimes even hats! Never try to do a high kick or big jump when cold, as something may 'snap'!

## SEW SIMPLE

1 Bend the heel of the shoe forward. Where it meets the side of the shoe is the right place to fix your elastic.

2 Sew on the elastic (without sewing through the drawstring). Put the shoe on to measure the elastic across and then do the other side.

1

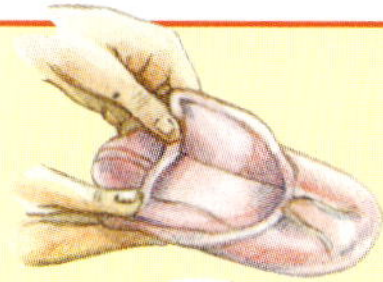

2

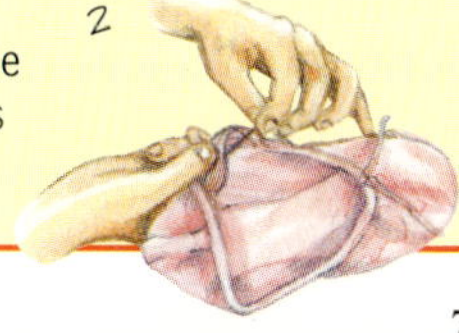

# Ready to Dance

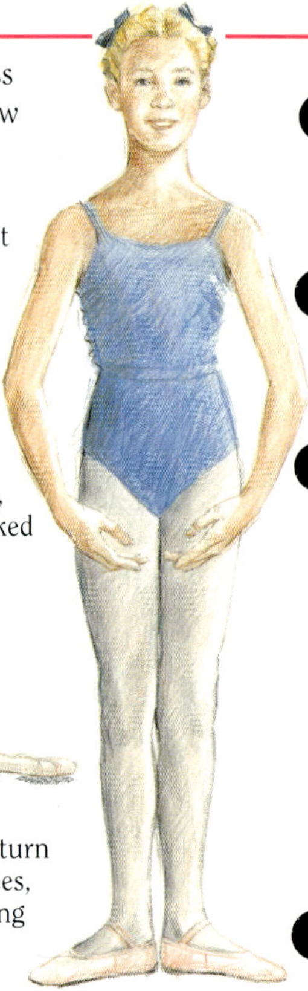

So, you have found the right class and the right clothes, you are now ready to dance!

**Perfect posture**
The first thing to learn is the 'correct stance' or how to stand properly. Think of your body as the letter 'I': tall, thin and straight, with nothing sticking out! To start with you might look more like the letter 'S' but with practice you will be able to stand with your weight centred (nose over toes), your legs pulled up, your tummy lifted, your bottom tucked under you, your shoulders down and your neck lengthened.

**Terrific turn out**
Your legs must be 'turned out'. The turn out starts from the hips, not the knees, and has to be learned gradually. Doing the splits will help you to improve your flexibility.

## POSITIONS OF THE FEET

There are five basic positions of the feet, although to begin with small children only learn the first two. In each position, the legs must be fully turned out. It was King Louis XIV's dancing teacher, Pierre Beauchamp, who first worked out the five positions. You can find out more about King Louis XIV on page 18.

FIRST: heels together and toes pointed away from each other.

1

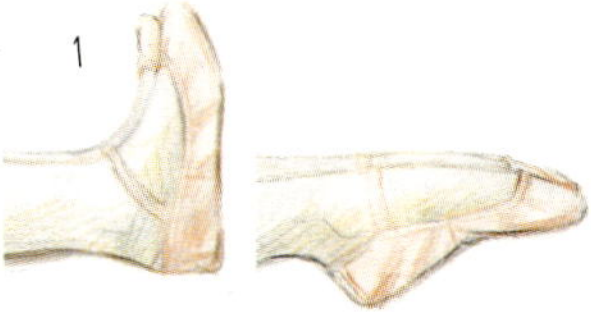

**Warming up**

1 Sit on the floor with your back straight and your legs out in front of you. Flex and point your feet.

2 Draw your feet up close to your body, gently let your knees flop to the side, urging them, but not forcing them, to go a little further. One day, they should be flat on the ground!

2

3

3 Stand with your feet apart but with your toes pointing forward. Stretch both arms up then forward and flop down to the floor. Slowly roll back up – and repeat.

## FOOTBALLET!

Believe it or not, the exercises footballers use to warm up are very similar to ballet!

**... and cooling down**

At the end of class, however hot and exhausted you are, give your muscles time to cool down before you collapse.

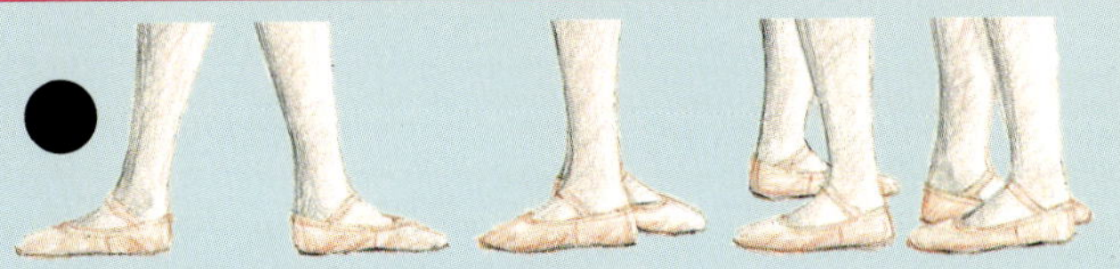

SECOND: like first but with the heels placed about 30cm apart.

THIRD: the heel of one foot is placed against the middle of the other.

FOURTH: one foot is placed in front of the other with a gap between.

FIFTH: the heel of one foot is placed beside the toe of the other.

# At the Barre

After you have warmed up, you're ready to begin the class at the 'barre'. The barre is a long pole used for balance and support. If there isn't a barre handy, the back of a chair may be used – or any solid piece of furniture of the right height.

**Stretching out**

At the end of the barre exercises when your muscles are warm, you can use the barre to help stretch your legs even more.

**Practising pliés**

Face the barre in first position. Keeping heels on the floor, bend your knees to the side. (Remember not to stick out your tail!) This is called a demi-plié. Let the heels come off the floor as your knees go wider and lower. This is a grand plié. In second position, you keep your heels on the floor at all times.

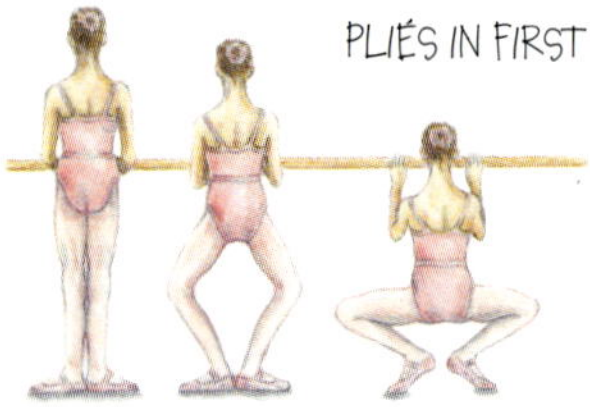

## DÉVELOPPÉS

As in grands battements, do not try to lift your leg too high too soon, otherwise some dreadful mistakes may occur!

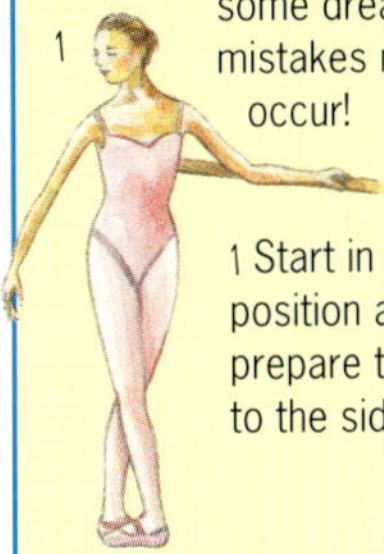

1 Start in fifth position and prepare the arm to the side.

2 Begin to draw the foot up to retiré (on the knee) trying to keep the knee to the side.

3 Stretch the leg out in front (devant) or to the side (à la seconde). Do not let your hips twist to the side.

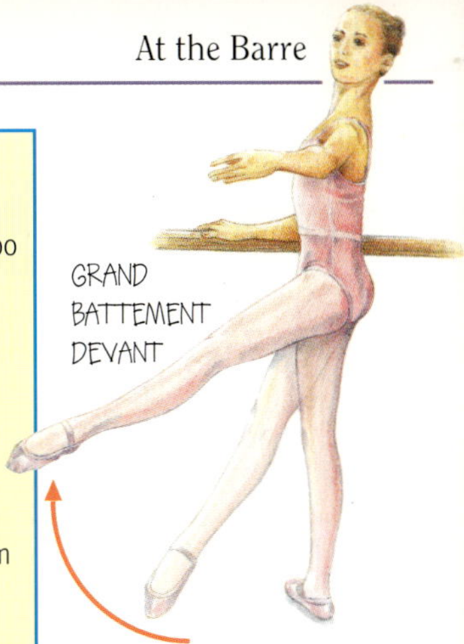

GRAND BATTEMENT DEVANT

**Great grands battements**
Younger children learn this first in four movements: point, kick, point and close. Older students use two movements: brush – point – kick followed by lower – point – close. Be careful not to bend the supporting leg.

**Battements tendus**
This is the best exercise for warming up your feet. You can start in first, third or fifth. Push the foot along the floor until the heel has to come up, then point your toe as much as possible. Relax the foot and return to the starting position. Really feel the floor under your foot as you close.

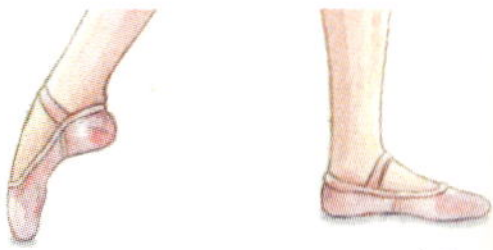

# In the Centre

When you've finished all the exercises at the barre, it's time to move into the middle of the studio for 'centre practice'. You will start with slow exercises (adage) and progress to quicker work (allegro) before finally tackling the big jumps (grands jetés).

**Ports de bras**
Arm exercises are known as ports de bras. The dancer concentrates on the upper part of her body, co-ordinating the use of her head, shoulders and arms. A dancer must never let her arms show – by straining – how hard she is working!

**Feeling dizzy!**
Fouetter means to whip, and the dancer spins on one leg while the other leg whips out and in. In some ballets the ballerina has to do 32 fouettés but the record is 166 turns without stopping!

**The secret of the perfect pirouette**
To perform good pirouettes you have to practise, practise and practise! For a pirouette en dehors (going outwards) try not to think of turning at first. From the fifth position relever (rise) strongly onto one leg, bringing the front toe to the knee (retiré) while at the same time pushing the knee back. Hold the arms en avant (in front), spot the front with your eyes – spin – and finish in a good plié with the foot behind.

**Handy hints**

Hands should never be rigid; always soft and delicate. When you stretch your fingers, you should feel as if they could stretch for ever!

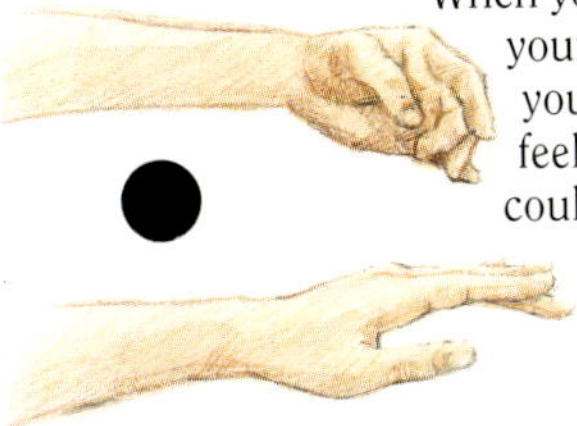

## THE LOW DOWN ON HIGH JUMPS

Can you pat a ball? The harder you pat it – (push it into the ground) – the higher the ball will bounce. In the same way, the deeper you plier into the floor – the higher you will be able to jump.

**The art of the arabesque**

Arabesques are first learned with both feet à terre (on the ground). Later on the leg is lifted at the back – higher and higher. A good 'line' in arabesques is essential.

ARABESQUE EN FONDU

**Alignment**

Dancers must always know which way they are facing. Imagine you are standing in the middle of a square, in fifth position with your right foot in front. Straight in front of you is en face. Point the front foot to one corner – on your left. This is croisé. If you point your front foot to the corner on your right the position is éffacé. In the écarté position, the legs, arm and head are all aligned, pointing to the side.

CROISÉ

ÉFFACÉ

ÉCARTÉ

# Jumps

All dancers have to develop a good jump – ballon. As the strength in your foot and leg muscles increases, you'll be able to jump higher.

**From simple skips...**
Not all jumps are as big as this grand jeté. There are also many variations of small, very quick jumps. The first jumping step everyone learns is skipping. If you can skip well – with high knees, stretched legs and pointed toes – it will help you learn the more difficult jumps.

## SUPER SAUTÉS

A sauté is a simple jump.

1 Start in first position with a demi-plié.

2 Push the floor away as you jump and *stretch* those feet!

3 Land softly, with your toes first, and finish in the starting position.

You can do sautés in second (and in any other position, too). Remember to always start and land with a good plié.

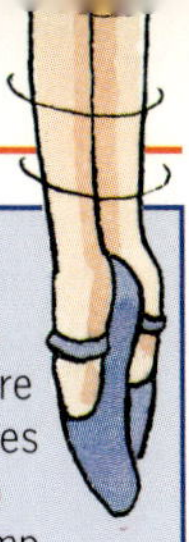

### Sissonnes made simple

1 Start with a demi-plié in fifth position.
2 Jump to the side and stretch both legs.
3 Land on the right leg (in a plié) and close the left foot in front to fifth position.

## HIGH FLYER

Entrechat quatre is a beating step, where the front foot crosses behind and back to the front as you jump. Wayne Sleep, a famous British dancer, once jumped so high that he executed an entrechat douze (crossing the legs five times). He was in the air for 0.71 seconds.

### Astounding assemblés

Assemblés are quite hard to do well. You start and finish with both feet in the fifth position. Brush your back foot to the second position, (still in demi-plié), then jump and stretch both feet. In the air, bring your front foot to meet the back foot, and then land on a plié in fifth position. You can also brush the front foot to the side and close behind.

## PAS DE CHAT

This is the 'step of the cat'. Start with the right foot behind in fifth. Demi-plié with your right arm bent en avant and your left arm in demi-seconde. Now pick up the back foot to retiré, jump, and bring the front foot up to meet the back foot. Close the back foot first followed by the front foot. So it's up, up, down, down!

# Sur les Pointes

Ever since the days when ladies like Marie Taglioni were the first to thrill audiences by performing steps on the tips of their toes, dancing 'sur les pointes' has become the ultimate ambition of all young girls in a ballet class.

MARIE TAGLIONI

**Be careful!**
Even if you are *longing* to go on pointes, do not do so until your teacher thinks you are ready. You need to be at least 11 years old, and should have worked hard at your ballet classes for several years. Starting any sooner could result in injury, which might spoil your dancing career for ever.

## LOOK AFTER YOUR POINTE SHOES

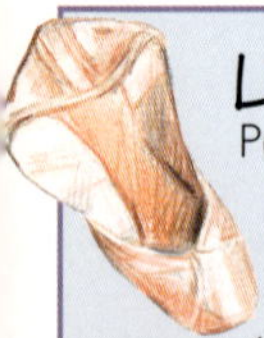

Pointe shoes are expensive, and must be cared for well. When they are new you should darn the blocks to help them last longer. Sew the ribbons on carefully and securely (turn the back of the shoe forward to find the right place). Everyone's feet are different – so it may take a while to find the best shoes to suit your feet.

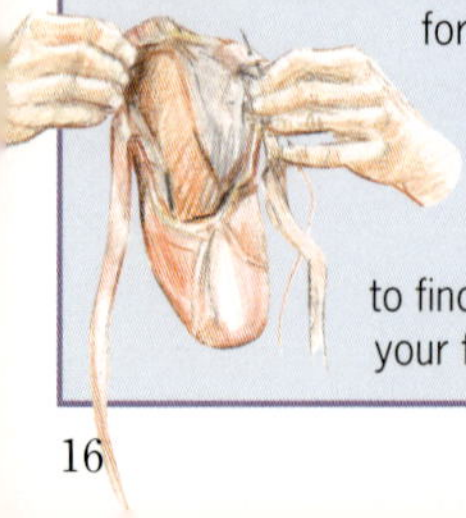

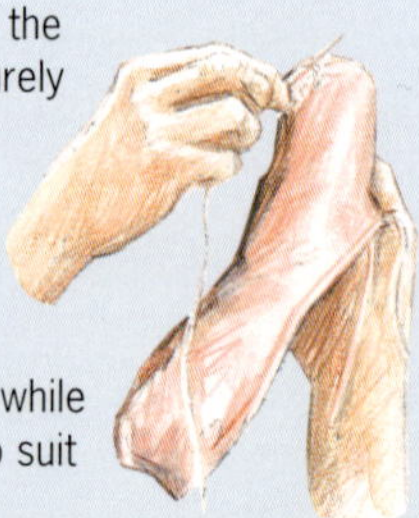

### Pas de bourrée

A good first step to learn on pointe. 1 Face the barre with your right foot behind, on the ankle and your left leg in demi-plié. 2 Step on to the right pointe, lifting the left leg to the front. 3 Step on to the left pointe, lifting the right leg in front. 4 Land on the right leg (in demi-plié) with the left leg behind.

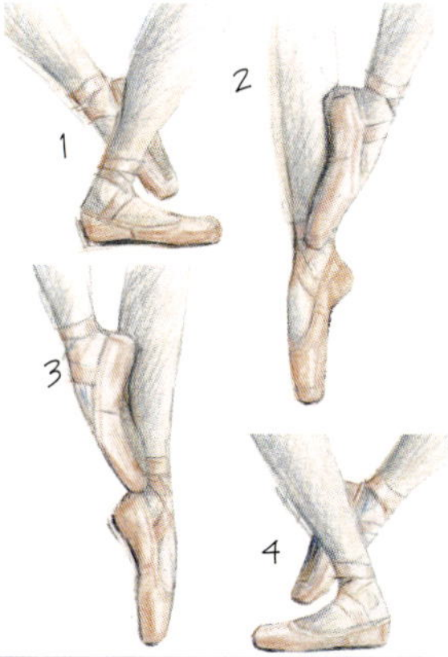


### Keep busy boys!

While the girls are doing pointe work, the boys do some different exercises to build up strength in their arms and shoulders. They will then be able to catch and hold ballerinas safely when dancing a pas de deux (dance for two people).

### Ouch!

Ballet is very demanding and can even be quite painful. Many toes have bled before the skin has become tough enough to cope with pointe shoes! You can help your feet by dabbing them with surgical spirit every day.

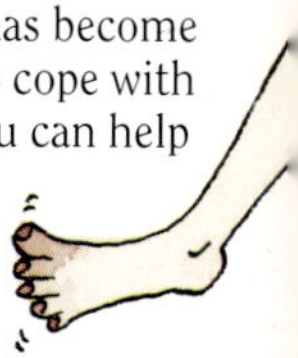

## TYING RIBBONS

1 Take one ribbon and, keeping it flat, cross it over the foot and behind the ankle. 2 Bring it round to the front again, quite firmly but not too tightly. 3 Do the same with the second ribbon.
4 Finish with a neat double knot on the inside of your foot. You should have enough ribbon left over to tuck the ends in tidily.

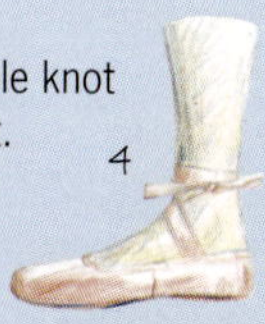

# Ballet History

People have danced since ancient times, but ballet as we know it really started in 1661, when the Académie Royale de Danse was established in Paris. This explains why the language of ballet is French. King Louis X1V was himself a dancer and appeared in several performances.

GREEK DANCERS 1000BC

## MEN ONLY?

In the very early days only men were allowed to dance, so they had to pretend to be women as well! Women took to the stage in the early 18th century and when ballet entered its golden age in the 19th century, some of its most famous stars were women.

CARLOTTA GRISI (1818–1899)

LOUIS XIV (1638–1715) IN HIS BALLET COSTUME

***Russian ballet?***

Many of the world's best known dancers began their careers in Russia. However, the School of Russian Ballet was in fact founded by a Frenchman (Marius Petipa), a Swede (Christian Johansson), and an Italian (Enrico Cecchetti)!

**Les Ballets Russes**

In 1909 a Russian called Serge Diaghilev brought a season of ballets to Paris. It was so successful that he formed a permanent ballet company in France called Les Ballets Russes. Diaghilev attracted the best talent of his day to work for him. Pavlova, Nijinsky, Lifar, Markova and Dolin danced for him, Picasso designed his sets, and Stravinsky composed for him.

DIAGHILEV

PAVLOVA

## ANNA PAVLOVA

Anna Pavlova is famous to this day – especially for dancing 'The Dying Swan'. She performed all over the world, often to people who had never seen a ballet. To make sure we never forget her, an Australian chef created a fluffy meringue pudding in her honour and called it a Pavlova!

**All over the world**

In the 20th century dancers began to travel the world and teach where they could. Thanks to them there are now wonderful companies in many countries, including Australia, the USA, Britain, Japan, Canada, Israel, South Africa and countries in South America.

THE AUSTRALIAN BALLET

# Great Teachers

## TOP SCHOOLS
Some of the world's most famous ballet schools are: The Kirov and The Bolshoi (both in Russia), The Royal Ballet in Britain, The Paris Opéra in France and The New York City Ballet in the USA.

Through the years there have been many famous and amazing ballet teachers. One of the best known was Maestro Enrico Cecchetti. He not only taught great stars such as Pavlova and Nijinsky, but also devised his own syllabus which is still taught all over the world.

CECCHETTI WITH SERGE LIFAR

## BENESH NOTATION
Before Benesh notation was invented in 1955, ballets had to be learnt by heart and passed from generation to generation. Benesh notation looks like a musical score and is used to describe ballet movements. Its symbols show how high the hands and feet are held and whether they are in front of, behind or level with the body.

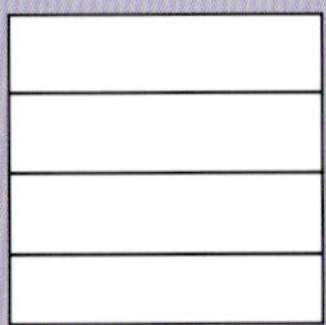


— hand or foot level with body

I hand or foot in front of body

● hand or foot behind body

+ knee or arm bent level with body

## Dame Ninette de Valois

The most influential lady in the ballet world for many years is called Dame Ninette de Valois. She was well known as a ballerina, then she became a teacher and founded the famous English ballet companies now known as the Royal Ballet Company and the Birmingham Royal Ballet.

*Ninette de Valois and some of her pupils.*

### *Right or wrong?*

The way ballet is taught varies from school to school. If, at the end of the day, a wonderful dancer is produced, who is to say what is right or wrong?

## TERRIFYING TEACHERS!

Often pupils used to be reduced to tears by their teachers shouting at them or using their canes rather painfully on legs that were incorrect! Under these conditions it would have been difficult to rehearse a dance full of joy and happiness!

# Famous Dancers

Many countries have produced famous ballet dancers. But some performers live on as legends. Without a doubt, the world's best known ballet partnership was that of Margot Fonteyn and Rudolph Nureyev.

**Dynamic duo**
Fonteyn was already a well-known prima ballerina with the Royal Ballet Company in Britain when a young dancer, named Rudolph Nureyev, moved from Russia in 1961. Although Fonteyn was 20 years older than Nureyev, the pair danced beautifully together, captivating audiences for many years.

FONTEYN AND NUREYEV

## FAME FOR WAYNE

Wayne Sleep is a brilliant and amazingly versatile British dancer. Not only have his leaps, turns and beats thrilled audiences everywhere, he has also produced his own successful shows.

WAYNE SLEEP IN CINDERELLA

## Stars from the East

Mikhail Barishnikov and Natalia Makarova were both born in Russia but preferred to dance in the West where they felt they had more freedom of expression.

BARISHNIKOV AND MAKAROVA

ERIK BRUHN

## Dancing Dane

When Erik Bruhn went on tour with the Royal Danish Ballet Company audiences knew they were watching a great star. He was the idol of many, including Rudolph Nureyev.

NIJINSKY

## Nijinsky

Vaslav Nijinsky died in 1950 but his legend lives on. He had a magical quality which combined his great artistic and balletic talents. When he jumped, he appeared to fly in the air like a bird.

## NAME DROPPING!

At one time it was thought better to have an exotic sounding name if you wanted to be a ballet star. So British dancers Peggy Hookham, Alice Marks and Patrick Kay became Margot Fonteyn, Alicia Markova and Anton Dolin!

# Old Favourites

It would be impossible to guess how often the great ballets have been performed since they were first created!

**A Christmas cracker!**
*The Nutcracker* is an enchanting fairy tale story of a little girl transported to the Kingdom of Sweets by a handsome prince one Christmas night. The solo danced by the Sugar Plum Fairy is one of the first dances that budding ballerinas learn.

## AVALANCHE!

A Boston Ballet production of *The Nutcracker* used more than one tonne of white confetti in the snow scene for 50 performances. Good thing it didn't all fall at once!

***Swan Lake***
In *Swan Lake* the ballerina has to dance two roles – Odette and Odile. 'The Dance of the Little Swans' is performed by four dancers: it is very fast and no one must make a mistake!

## PANTO BALLETS

Believe it or not, certain comic female roles are danced by men. In *La Fille Mal Gardée*, Lise's mother, who performs an amusing clog dance, is always a man. And in *Cinderella* the ugly 'sisters' are not quite what they seem!

***Living doll?***

In *Coppélia* an old toy maker creates a beautiful life-sized doll of which he is very proud. One of the villagers plays a trick on the old man by dressing up as the doll so that he thinks his Coppélia really has come to life.

COPPÉLIA

**A tragic tale**

*Giselle* is a romantic ballet. Duke Albrecht falls in love with Giselle, a peasant girl and disguises himself as a villager so he can court her. But the duke is already engaged and when Giselle discovers this she goes mad and kills herself with Albrecht's sword. Giselle becomes a spirit, or Wili. When Duke Albrecht comes to her grave, Giselle shows that she still loves him by protecting him from the cruel Wili queen.

DUKE ALBRECHT AT GISELLE'S GRAVE

**Ballet music**

Many composers have written scores for ballets which have become famous pieces of music. Tchaikovsky (1840–1893) wrote memorable music for *The Nutcracker*, *Swan Lake* and *The Sleeping Beauty*.

TCHAIKOVSKY

# Creating New Ballet

We must thank choreographers past and present for their creative talents in putting together the steps and movements that make a ballet.

*Modern ballets are often abstract.*

**Petipa**
It is amazing to think that although he died in 1910, Marius Petipa's steps and creations are still being danced today. Among his most famous ballets are *Don Quixote* (1869) and *La Bayadère* (1877).

**Balanchine in action**
When Balanchine's work was first seen outside the USA, people marvelled at how modern and different it was. His brilliance in giving classical dance a new dimension lives on to this day.

***Ballet battle***
*The exciting sword fight in Romeo and Juliet has been very carefully choreographed.*

*A poster advertising the Ballets Russes' season for 1912.*

**The shock of the new**
In the early 1900s people started to experiment with new forms of choreography. Diaghilev's Ballets Russes company ignored criticism from traditionalists and proudced ballets like *The Firebird*. With music composed by Stravinsky, it was a sensation.

*The Dance Theater of Harlem performing* Stars and Stripes.

**Modern companies**
There are many dance companies today, like the Ballet Rambert in the UK, dedicated to modern or experimental ballet. In the USA, the Dance Theater of Harlem and the Alvin Ailey Dance Company are two companies composed only of black dancers. Their exciting, vibrant and beautiful dancing brings a new dimension to ballet.

## I WANT A NEW BALLET!

It is considered the height of honour for a ballet to be especially created for a single ballerina. Recently Kenneth Macmillan created a ballet for Darcey Bussell, prima ballerina with the Royal Ballet Company. It is called *Winter Dreams*.

# Style on Stage

Gone are the days when costumes were hot, heavy and cumbersome! Today we can be dazzled by amazing costumes that sparkle, shine or even change colour!

ONE OF BAKST'S DESIGNS

**Design gurus**

Set and costume designers can be as famous as the dancers, choreographers and composers. If they happened to be called Pablo Picasso or Leon Bakst, people sometimes went to the ballet just to admire their designs!

***Is it art?***

In 1917 a new ballet called *Parade* was staged. Picasso's 'cubist' costume designs certainly caused a stir.

## DID YOU KNOW?

The short stiffened skirt worn by ballerinas surprised audiences so much when it first appeared that the word tutu comes from the French slang word 'cucul' which means silly! Tutus hang upside down for storage. This protects the delicate layers of the skirt and bodice.

**Fashion frog**

Not only does *The Tales of Beatrix Potter* have the most wonderful music by John Launchberry and superb choreography by Kenneth MacMillan, but the costumes are so brilliant, they make a show on their own! Here's Jeremy Fisher, leaping over the lily pads.

**Making faces**

A dancer's make-up does not look very flattering, but on stage, under the bright lights, it looks quite normal. Make-up is even more important if the dancer is portraying a character such as an animal or a doll.

## MIME QUIZ

Mime is a must to help tell the story in a ballet. Here are some mime actions – see if you can guess what they are.

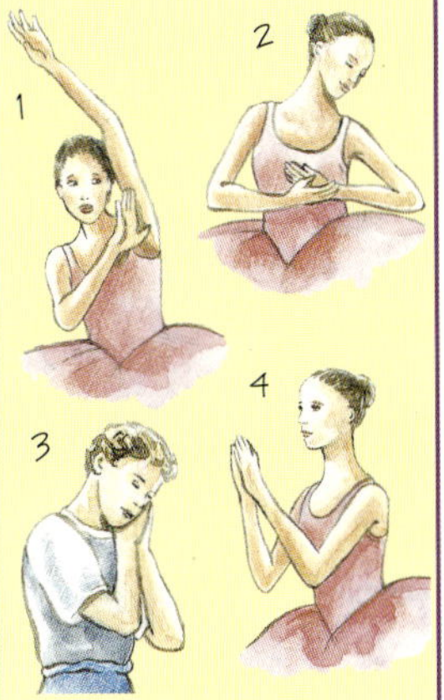


Answers:
1 Fright
2 Love
3 Sleep (for men)
4 Beg

# It's Showtime

Putting on a show is hard work. Here's a countdown to curtain up!

*Before the dances are taught to the cast, the music is composed and the movements have to be choreographed.*

*The pianist learns the music and the teacher will cover the new steps in class. Meanwhile costumes, scenery and props are made, a venue is found and the lighting and everything backstage is organised.*

*At the dress rehearshal things usually go wrong! But you have to expect mishaps because it's first time everyone has been in costume.*

*'Putting on the greasepaint' as the show approaches is very exciting. Younger children are made up by older cast members.*

*The dances have been learnt, the rehearsals are over, everyone's dressed and made up, the music has begun... it's time for the curtain to go up!*

**Bravo!**

When you're on the stage, in front of an appreciative audience, it makes all those weeks of hard work worthwhile. If you join a ballet company, you must be prepared to perform almost every night, often rehearsing another show during the day. Companies on tour sometimes perform in very unusual venues, such as the Hollywood Bowl football stadium in California or even under canvas in Africa.

## BORED?

You have to rehearse and rehearse for a show. You won't be needed all the time but it doesn't have to be boring. You can learn a lot by watching others.

*In ballet the bow (for boys) and curtsey (for girls) is known as the révérence. It is the traditional way for a dancer to thank the teacher at the end of a class.*

**Take a bow**

Imagine it – what a great moment! The show is behind you and you know you have danced your very best. All the hard work, pain and anguish is now forgotten as, listening to the thunderous applause, you take your bow!

# INDEX

Alignment ....................13
Arabesques ....................13
Assemblés ....................15
Bakst, Leon ....................28
Balanchine, George ....................26
Ballet clothes ....................6–7, 28
Ballets Russes ....................19, 27
Barishnikov, Mikhail ....................23
Barre ....................10–11
Benesh notation ....................20–21
Bruhn, Erik ....................23
Bussell, Darcey ....................27
Cecchetti, Enrico ....................18, 20
Choreography ....................26–27, 28, 30
*Cinderella* ....................22, 25
*Coppélia* ....................25
Corps de ballet ....................2
Costumes ....................28–29, 30
Développés ....................11
Diaghilev, Serge ....................19
Dolin, Anton ....................23
Feet positions ....................8–9
*Firebird, The* ....................27
Flat shoes ....................6–7
Fonteyn, Dame Margot ....................3, 22, 23
Fouettés ....................12
*Giselle* ....................25
Grands battements ....................11
Grands jetés ....................14
Hair ....................7
Hands ....................13
History of ballet ....................18–19
Jetés ....................4
Jumps ....................13, 14–15
*La Fille Mal Gardée* ....................25
Louis XIV ....................8, 18
MacMillan, Kenneth ....................27, 29
Makarova, Natalia ....................23
Make-up ....................29, 30
Markova, Alicia ....................23
Mime ....................29
Modern ballet ....................26–27
Nijinsky, Vaslav ....................20, 23
Nureyev, Rudolph ....................3, 4, 22
*Nutcracker, The* ....................24, 25
Pas de bourrée ....................17
Pas de chat ....................15
Pavlova, Anna ....................19, 20
Petipa, Marius ....................18, 26
Picasso, Pablo ....................28
Pirouettes ....................13
Pliés ....................4, 10, 17
Pointe shoes ....................6, 16–17
Ports de bras ....................4, 12
Posés ....................4
Posture ....................8
Premier danseur ....................2
Prima ballerina ....................2, 27
Relevés ....................4
*Romeo and Juliet* ....................26
Royal Ballet Company ....................20, 22, 27
Sautés ....................4, 14
Sissonnes ....................15
Sleep, Wayne ....................3, 15, 22
*Sleeping Beauty, The* ....................25
*Swan Lake* ....................3, 24, 25
Taglioni, Marie ....................16
*Tales of Beatrix Potter, The* ....................29
Tchaikovsky ....................25
Teachers ....................5, 20–21
Tendus ....................4, 11
Turn out ....................8
Valois, Ninette de ....................21
Warming up ....................7, 8–9
*Winter Dreams* ....................27



Written by Elfrida Eden
Designed by Brian Robins and Jacqueline Palmer

First published in 1996 by HarperCollins Children's Books,
A Division of HarperCollins Publishers Ltd, 77–85 Fulham Palace Road, London W6 8JB

ISBN: 0 00 197959 0

Illustrations: Amy Burch, Charlotte Hard, Christian Hook, Tamara Sternberg

Photographs: Dee Conway 27b, Bill Cooper 25tr; Zoë Dominic 4, 24, 25bl; E.T. Archive 18, 27t; Hulton Deutsch 16, 19tr, 21, 23tl, 25br, 26cl; Mander & Mitchenson 20; Mansell Collection 23b; Performing Arts Library/ Jane Mont 26tr; Popperfoto 7, 19tl; Royal Opera House 26cr; Leslie E. Spatt 19b, 26b, 29; The Theatre Museum 28b; Victoria and Albert Museum 28t; Reg Wilson 22t & B, 23tr.





A CIP record for this book is available from the British Library

Printed and bound in Hong Kong